PICZART

THIS RACE CAR IS FAST!

CLINE MCKINLEY BAKER

The red car is fast.

The orange car is fast.

3

4

The yellow car is fast.

The green car is fast.

5

The blue car is fast.

The purple car is fast.

7

The pink car is fast.

The brown car is fast.

9

The **black** car is fast.

The white car is fast.

The silver car is fast.

The gold car is fast.

13

The green car is fast.

The pink car wins!

blue

green

pink

yellow

16